AS Ethics

Revision Guide for AQA Religion and Ethics Unit A (RSS01)

Peter Baron & Liam Spencer

Published by Inducit Learning Ltd,

Mid Somerset House, Southover, Wells

Somerset BA5 1UH United Kingdom

www.pushmepress.com

First published in 2011, second edition 2012

ISBN: 978-1-910038-69-7

Issues arising summarised in each section are taken from the AQA specification (RST 3A) copyright AQA 2014.

Contents

How to Get an A Grade

Effective learning involves reducing difficult topics into smaller, "bite-sized" chunks.

Every revision guide, card or study guide from PushMe Press comes with its own website consisting of summaries, handouts, games, model essays, revision notes and more. Each website community is supported by the best teachers in the country.

At the end of each chapter you will see an `i-pu-sh` web link that you can type into your web browser along with a QR code that can be scanned by our free App.

These links will give you immediate access to the additional resources you need to "Get an A Grade" by providing you with the relevant information needed.

Getting an A Grade has never been easier.

Download our FREE How to Get an A Grade in Ethics App for your phone or tablet and get up-to-date information that accompanies this book and the whole PushMe Press range.

http://ethics.pushmepress.com/download

Acknowledgment

I am grateful to Henry Swales for permission to include in this guide original material from his revision summary sheets first developed for his students at Tonbridge School, Kent.

Syllabus

UNIT A

The syllabus specifies four topics, and requires us to answer one question. In each section, however, there is no choice of question - as only one is set. This suggests we need a thorough knowledge of the logic of each moral theory and how it might apply to ethical cases. We then answer **TWO** questions from the choice of four.

The four areas are:

1. **UTILITARIANISM**

2. **SITUATION ETHICS**

3. **RELIGIOUS TEACHING ON THE NATURE AND VALUE OF HUMAN LIFE**

4. **ABORTION** and **EUTHANASIA**

The examiner asks us to think **SYNOPTICALLY**. This means we should think of the syllabus as a whole where each part relates to the other. This is helped by the fact that forms of utilitarianism and Christian situation ethics are both **TELEOLOGICAL**, meaning that the goodness of an action is related to the **END** (telos). The strong advice is to study the whole syllabus and then relate different parts to each other, even though on the day of the exam we only need to answer a question from two of the four topic areas.

The syllabus also encourages us to think **ANALYTICALLY** and **CRITICALLY**. There are many different views of the validity, for example, of situation ethics or utilitarianism. There are many views on the ethics of **ABORTION** (women's rights, sanctity of life and consequentialist views for example). We need to study each topic in depth to bring out these different approaches. Read around the topics and be prepared to quote from different philosophers.

Try to disentangle the moral **PRINCIPLES** at the heart of each theory from their application (see final chapter on the four questions posed in the introductory chapter). When we apply the principles, we need to study not just the designated two applied areas of **ABORTION** and **EUTHANASIA,** but also one other area of our choice. For this reason the optional area of **GENETIC ENGINEERING** is included in this study guide.

Introduction to Ethics

NORMATIVE ETHICS

Asks the question "how should I act, morally speaking?" or "what ought I to do?" Normative ethics seeks to extract **MORAL PRINCIPLES** from theories of ethics and then apply them to real-world cases.

A norm is a "value," meaning "something I think of as good." The normative theories we study at AS are Utilitarianism and Christian Situation Ethics.

APPLIED ETHICS

Applies ethical theories to real world situations. The applied issues at AS (AQA) are:

- **ABORTION**

- **EUTHANASIA**

- **AN ETHICAL ISSUE OF YOUR CHOICE**

DEONTOLOGICAL

Acts are right or wrong in themselves (intrinsically) - it is not about consequences. Often stresses the rules or duties (Kantian ethics and Natural Law, for example, are not studied in Unit A, but are studied in detail in Unit B). **DEON** is Greek for duty.

TELEOLOGICAL

Teleological theories (**TELOS** = end in Greek) focuses on consequences of actions. An action is good only if it brings about beneficial consequences (it is instrumentally good, not intrinsically because actions are means to some other end like happiness or pleasure) for example, Utilitarianism and Situation Ethics. This syllabus is based on a study of **TELEOLOGICAL ETHICS** where goodness is related to the end or purpose of an action.

Four questions to ask of moral theories:

- **DERIVATION** - How does the moral theory derive (produce) the idea of goodness?

- **APPLICATION** - How can we apply the "good" to choices we make?

- **REALISM** - How realistic is the theory?

- **MOTIVATION** - Why should I be moral?

These questions will be answered for all moral theories in the final chapter.

Bentham's Act Utilitarianism

BENTHAM (1748-1832) was a social reformer who believed that the law should serve human needs and welfare. Where **JUSTICE** was **RETRIBUTIVE** he wanted to see it **REFORMING** and acting as a **DETERRENCE** - there had to be a real social benefit outweighing the pain to the criminal, and with a better **DISTRIBUTION** of resources, but all in the cause of the **GREATEST HAPPINESS PRINCIPLE (GHP)** - the motive was to reduce suffering and increase happiness for everyone. The theory is **TELEOLOGICAL** because it measures likely consequences of **ACTIONS**, and **HEDONIC** because Bentham believed pleasure (Greek: hedon) was the key motive and could be quantified. So there is an **EMPIRICAL**, objective measure of goodness.

MOTIVATION

There is one **MORAL** good - pleasure, and one evil - pain. "Nature has placed mankind under two **SOVEREIGN** masters, pain and pleasure." Right actions are on balance pleasurable, wrong actions are on balance painful. Bentham's is therefore a theory of **PSYCHOLOGICAL HEDONISM** (Hedonism - pleasure-seeking).

HEDONIC CALCULUS

The **HEDONIC CALCULUS** is a way of measuring pleasure and pain, so the consequences of an act can be assessed as a score in units of happiness called **HEDONS** (plus for pleasure, minus for pain). The seven criteria are (acronym **PRRICED**): **P**urity, **R**ichness, **R**eliability, **I**ntensity, **C**ertainty, **E**xtent, **D**uration. In this assessment "everyone is to count as one and no-one as more than one" (Bentham) so there is strict **EQUALITY**.

QUANTITATIVE PLEASURE

Bentham believed "pushpin is as good as poetry" (pushpin - a pub game equivalent to playing a slot machine in today's terms). Pleasure is purely **QUANTITATIVE** so we can't award more hedons to listening to Mozart or painting a picture or grasping philosophy. Mill, who was saved from mental breakdown by **WORDSWORTH'S** poetry, really objected to this. According to Bentham, we can compare a small child's delight in a new toy with someone else's delight in a new girlfriend. A **PIG** enjoying a good wallow is of more value than **SOCRATES** having a sightly sad think. Hence why critics call it "the pig philosophy."

PLEASURE MACHINES

JCC SMART (1973:18-21) asks us to imagine a pleasure machine where we can be wired up every day and passively enjoy every pleasure imaginable (note - addiction often operates like this as a kind of refuge in a supposed pleasure - like drink). **ALDOUS HUXLEY** wrote of a brave new world where people popped **SOMA** tablets to make them happy (there were 41 million antidepressant prescriptions in the UK in 2012). Bentham can have no problems with this, but **MILL** saw happiness as a wider idea involving **ACTIVITY**, and realistic goals and expectations (closer to what my therapist might advise or what **ARISTOTLE** argues).

STRENGTHS

- **SIMPLICITY** - There is a simplicity of application of utilitarianism and in Betham's calculation. The moral theory is really easy to use and so all people can engage with the moral theory and apply it in their lives.

- **COMMON SENSE** - The moral judgements of Bentham's utilitarianism fit with with our commonsense view of morality.

- **NOT ELITIST** - In his statement "pushpin is equal to poetry" Bentham makes it clear that morality should not be elitist. All people and their own conception of pleasure are included equally in their moral decision making.

- **YARDSTICK** - Bentham's utilitarianism can act as a method of measuring the impact a new law could have on society. By comparing it against utilitarianism, MPs can check whether or not the new law would be beneficial for the majority of people. For example, consider the debate proceeding the **ABORTION ACT** of 1967 - it is much easier to make the hedonic calculation looking backwards at the past than looking forwards.

WEAKNESSES

- **COUNTER INTUITIVE CONSEQUENCES** - Because Bentham believes that all pleasure is equal it can lead to counterintuitive consequences. For example, doctors in a hospital when faced with an organ shortage could justify killing one healthy patient to save the lives (and increase the pleasure) of five people.

- **MEASURING PLEASURE** - How is possible to measure pleasure? Pleasure is a subjective concept and what one person considers pleasurable might not be the same as another.

- **NO RULES** - Bentham focuses only on **ACTIONS** so we have to keep on calculating each moral situation. (He doesn't allow us to have general rules which does make life easier).

- **PLEASURE MACHINE** - Bentham has no answer for JCC Smart's **PLEASURE MACHINE** or Huxley's **SOMA** tablet in Brave New World,(of course, they were writing two centuries later so even if his stuffed skeleton, residing in a cupboard in London University, could talk, we don't know what it would say!). If pleasure is so important why don't we just take a pill to keep us happy at all times?

KEY QUOTES

1. *"Nature has placed mankind under two sovereign masters, pain and pleasure. It is for them to point out what we ought to do as well as determine what we should do."* Jeremy Bentham

2. *"In every human breast, self-regarding interest is predominant over social interest; each person's own individual interest over the interests of all other persons taken together."* Jeremy Bentham, Book of Fallacies, p 392

3. *"The community is a fictitious body,"* and it is but *"the sum of the interests of the several members who compose it."* Jeremy Bentham

4. *"Prejudice apart, the game of pushpin is of equal value with the arts and sciences of music and poetry. If the game of pushpin furnishes more pleasure, it is more valuable than either."* Jeremy Bentham

GET MORE HELP

Get more help with Bentham's act utilitarianism by using the links below:

http://i-pu.sh/H5G60N85

Mill's Rule Utilitarianism

The weak **RULE UTILITARIANISM** (RU) of John Stuart Mill (1806-73) is a **TELEOLOGICAL** (telos = goal) theory based on a definition of goodness as the **BALANCE** of happiness over misery. This is a measurable, **EMPIRICAL** idea - measure the happiness effects of likely consequences - giving an **OBJECTIVE** measure of goodness. Mill was against the **INTUITIONISTS** which he found too **SUBJECTIVE**. Mill argues that happiness is most likely to be maximised by generally following a set of **RULES** which society has found, by experience, maximise utility. But the rules can develop and in cases of moral dilemmas, we should revert to being **ACT UTILITARIANS** (AU), OR weak **RULE UTILITARIANS** (RU) because the rules aren't absolute, but are **GUIDELINES**.

MILL vs BENTHAM

Mill disliked three aspects of **BENTHAM'S** version:

1. The implications of categorising all pleasures as of equal value - drinking beer vs listening to Mozart.

2. The emphasis on pleasure alone, as Mill was influenced by **ARISTOTLE'S** views on virtue (eg the importance of **SYMPATHY** for others).

3. The problem of **JUSTICE** and **RIGHTS** - how do we prevent one innocent person or group being sacrificed for the general happiness of the majority? So Mill devotes the last chapter of his essay to **JUSTICE**.

Mill on Happiness

Mill's definition of a happy life has three elements - **PLEASURE** (varied and rich) and absence of pain, **AUTONOMY** (the free choice of a life goal), and **ACTIVITY** (motivated by virtues like sympathy eg Mill used to hand out leaflets advising about contraception and campaigned for women's rights).

> "HAPPINESS is not a life of rapture, but moments of such, in an existence with few and transitory pains, many and various pleasures, with a decided predominance of the ACTIVE over the passive, and having as a foundation of the whole, not to expect more from life than it is capable of bestowing." JS Mill

Higher and Lower Pleasures

Mill was saved from a nervous breakdown in his 20s by the **ROMANTIC MOVEMENT** eg Wordsworth's Lyrical Ballads. To him poetry was infinitely superior to **PUSHPIN**. So "better to be Socrates dissatisfied than a fool satisfied." The **LOWER** bodily pleasures (food, sex, drink, football) were of less value than the **HIGHER** pleasures (reading, thinking, listening to Mozart). So Mill followed **ARISTOTLE** in seeing education as of vital importance (the supreme Greek value is **CONTEMPLATION** to gain wisdom). Only a person who'd experienced both could really judge the difference in **QUALITY** (so we say qualitative pleasure is superior to quantitative). He called those who hadn't experienced both "inferior beings." Does this make Mill a snob?

Rules

Mill has been called an "inconsistent utilitarian" (Alasdair MacIntyre) - because as his essay goes on he moves from **ACT** to **RULE** utilitarianism. We use generations of **PAST EXPERIENCE** to form rules, so we don't have to do a calculation to know whether **MURDER** or **THEFT** is "right." We inherit **BELIEFS** "and the beliefs which have thus come down are the **RULES** of morality for the multitude" (JS Mill). These are not fixed but "admit of continual improvement" - so not **ABSOLUTE**. The **FIRST PRINCIPLE** is utility (or the Greatest Happiness Principle) and then **SECONDARY PRINCIPLES** (rules) come from this and are constantly evaluated against the first principle. Just as navigation is based on astronomy doesn't mean the sailor goes back to the stars every time - no, Mill reminds us, he uses an **ALMANAC** - so, argues Mill, human beings follow a code book of rules passed down from previous generations as the best way to be happy.

Justice

Bernard **WILLIAMS** argued that Utilitarianism violates our **MORAL INTEGRITY** by encouraging us to do things we would find repulsive - like his example of Jim who is invited to kill one Indian as an honoured guest in order to save 19 others. This is the problem of **INJUSTICE** - the Southern States may have enjoyed lynching innocent people in the 1920s but this doesn't make it right. Mill argues that unhappiness is caused by selfishness, by people "acting only for themselves," and that for a person to be happy they need "to cultivate a fellow feeling with the collective interests of mankind" and "in the **GOLDEN RULE** of Jesus we find the whole ethics of utility" (JS Mill). So we need to defend personal **RIGHTS** and "Justice is a name for certain moral requirements, which, regarded collectively, stand higher in the scale of **SOCIAL UTILITY**, and are therefore of more paramount obligation, than any others," and "justice is a name for certain classes of **MORAL RULES**, which concern the essentials of human **WELL-BEING**." Rights, justice and the virtue of sympathy stop selfish self-interest destroying the happiness of others. So we escape the problem of Jim and the Indians as we would never shoot one indian (violate their right to life) to save 19.

Act or Rule?

LOUIS POJMAN argues (2006:111) that we can adopt a **MULTILEVEL** approach (this is what Mill seems to be doing in talking about **PRIMARY** and **SECONDARY** principles). So we can have three levels if we wish: rules of thumb to live by which generally maximise utility, a second set of rules for resolving conflicts between these, and a third process - an **ACT** utilitarian one, for assessing a difficult situation according to the **GREATEST HAPPINESS PRINCIPLE** or GHP (eg lying to save a friend). But in this way philosophers like **JO URMSON** argue that **RULE** utilitarianism collapses into **ACT** utilitarianism. Mill might counter that we don't have the time, the wisdom, or the resources to keep calculating every action and this multilevel approach is therefore realistic and practical in a way that **KANT'S** deontology is unrealistic and impractical because it cannot handle **MORAL DILEMMAS**.

STRENGTHS

- **NO COUNTERINTUITIVE CONSEQUENCES** - Mill was particularly worried about the implications of counting all pleasure as equal. By introducing higher and lower pleasures Mill overcomes this problem.

- **RATIONALITY** - Utilitarian ethics rests on a personal calculation of number of people whose pleasure or happiness is maximised.

- **EQUALITY** - Equality is central. Bentham wrote "everyone is to count as one, and no-one as more than one." This radical idea implies that everyone has equal weight in the utility calculation. Mill adds equal rights. Suppose on an equal vote you all vote for my dismissal (or even death) in line with maximising general happiness? "The utilitarian emphasis on impartiality must be a part of any defensible moral theory." (Rachels, 2006:114). Finally, utilitarianism takes account of the **FUTURE** - issues of climate change, potential future wars and famines all suggest we need an ethical theory that takes into account those yet unborn.

- **COMMON SENSE** - The moral judgements of Mill's utilitarianism fit with with our commonsense view of morality. It makes sense that more moral worth should be attributed to some pleasures than others, and Mill's version of **RULE** utilitarianism argues that we should generally follow rules which wisdom has confirmed as practical, whilst reserving the right to become an **ACT** utilitarian if the situation demands it.

WEAKNESSES

- **PREDICTING THE FUTURE** - Utilitarians are required to predict the future when making decisions about morality. This is often very difficult as consequences are hard to predict.

- **ELITIST** - Mill says that the intellectual man is capable of making the true moral decision because he has experienced both types of pleasure. However, this seems to imply that only the most educated can be the most moral because they have experienced the best things in life. Am I less moral because I don't enjoy and appreciate Pushkin?

- **DOCTRINE OF NEGATIVE RESPONSIBILITY** - Bernard Williams claims that Utilitarianism implies a doctrine of negative responsibility. In the case of Jim and the Sadistic Guard, Jim appears to be morally responsible for the death of the prisoners even though he refused to kill a single person.

- **IGNORES SPECIAL RESPONSIBILITY** - **WD ROSS** claimed that because Utilitarianism is a single factor ethical theory (based on the **GREATEST HAPPINESS PRINCIPLE**) it can't take into account the special responsibility we have towards those in our care. Suppose we were to come across two people in the sea whilst we were in a lifeboat. One of them has the cure to HIV/AIDS and another is your son. Utilitarianism would agree you should save the man with the cure but most people would save their own son.

- **RATIONALITY** and **PRACTICALITY** - Utilitarian ethics rests on a rational calculation of numbers of people whose pleasure or happiness is maximised. There is a clarity and simplicity to this. **EQUALITY** is central. Bentham wrote "everyone is to count as one, and no-one as more than one." This radical idea implies that everyone has equal weight in the utility calculation. **MILL** adds equal **RIGHTS**. Suppose, on an equal vote, you all vote for my dismissal (or even death) in line with maximising general happiness? "The utilitarian emphasis on impartiality must be a part of any defensible moral theory," (Rachels, 2006:114). Finally, utilitarianism takes account of the **FUTURE** - issues of climate change, potential future wars and famines all suggest we need an ethical theory that takes into account those yet unborn.

KEY QUOTES - MILL'S UTILITARIANISM

1. *"It is better to be a human being dissatisfied than a pig satisfied; better Socrates dissatisfied than a fool satisfied."* JS Mill

2. *"Happiness is ... moments of rapture ... in an existence of few and transitory pains, many and various pleasures, with a predominance of the active over the passive ... not to expect more from life than it is capable of bestowing."* JS Mill

3. *"Whatever we adopt as the fundamental principle of Morality, we require subordinate principles to apply it by."* (Fundamental principle = happiness is good, subordinate principles = rules) JS Mill

4. *"By the improvement of education, the feeling of unity with our fellow-creatures shall be as deeply rooted in our character, and to our own consciousness as completely a part of our nature, as the horror of crime is in an ordinarily well brought up young person."* (= sympathy) JS Mill

5. *"To have a right, then, is, I conceive, to have something which society should defend me in possession of. If the objector asks why? I can give no other answer than general utility."* JS Mill

6. *"Justice is a name for certain moral requirements, which, regarded collectively, stand higher in the scale of social utility, and are therefore of more paramount obligation, than any others; though particular cases may occur in which some other social duty is so important as to overrule any one of the general maxims of justice. Thus to save a life it may not only be allowable, but a duty, to steal, or take by force, the necessary food or medicine, or to kidnap, or compel to officiate, the only qualified medical practitioner."* JS Mill (note - so RU collapses into AU)

7. *"I account the justice which is grounded on utility to be the chief part, and incomparably the most sacred and binding part, of all morality. Justice is a name for certain classes of moral rules, which concern the essentials of human well-being more nearly, and are therefore of more absolute obligation, than any other rules for the guidance of life." JS Mill*

8. *BERNARD WILLIAMS argues that "because our relation to the world is partly given by moral feelings, and by a sense of what we can or cannot "live with," to regard those feelings as happening outside one's moral self is to lose one's moral identity; to lose, in the most literal way, one's integrity." (Utilitarianism For and Against page 104)*

Confusions of Mill

1. Was Mill an Act or Rule Utilitarian? He is sometimes described as a **WEAK RULE UTILITARIAN**. Mill believed that generally we should follow the rule as this reflects society's view of what maximises happiness from past social experience. But when a pressing utilitarian need arises we should break the rule and so become an act utilitarian.

2. "Mill took Bentham's view that happiness equates to pleasure." Sometimes Mill seems to argue this, but it's truer to say Mill's view is close to **ARISTOTLE'S** that happiness means "personal and social flourishing." So to Mill the individual cannot be happy without the guarantee of certain rules and rights and clear goals to aim for.

Issues Arising from Utilitarianism *(exam board checklist)*

1. Strengths and weaknesses of the ethical systems of Bentham and Mill

2. Which is more important - the ending of pain and suffering, or the increase of pleasure?

3. How worthwhile is the pursuit of happiness, and is it all that people desire?

4. How compatible is Utilitarianism with a religious approach to ethics?

GET MORE HELP

Get more help with Mill's rule utilitarianism by using the links below:

http://i-pu.sh/B1V84G70

Situation Ethics - Christian Relativism

Situation Ethics is a **NORMATIVE** theory (tells you what is right/wrong - what you ought to do) that is **TELEOLOGICAL** and **CONSEQUENTIALIST** (acts are right or wrong if they bring about good/bad consequences, or can be seen as instrumentally good/bad) and **RELATIVIST** (there are no universal rules as actions depend on circumstances; there is just one general universal value - that of agape love). It is also **CHRISTIAN**, based on the principle of selfless sacrificial love (**AGAPE**).

INTRODUCTION

Joseph Fletcher (1966) argued there are three approaches to ethics:

1. **LEGALISTIC** - Someone who follows absolute rules and laws. Fletcher rejects this as it leads to **UNTHINKING OBEDIENCE** and needs elaborate systems of exceptions and compromises.

2. **ANTINOMIAN** - Nomos is Greek for law, so anti-law or someone who rejects all rules and laws (Fletcher rejects this as it would lead to social **CHAOS**).

3. **SITUATIONAL** - Fletcher argues that each individual situation is different and absolute rules are too demanding and restrictive. Instead we should decide what is the most **LOVING** course of action (**AGAPE**). The Situationist has respect for laws and tradition, but they are only guidelines to how to achieve this loving outcome, and thus they may be broken if the other course of action would result in more love.

However, Situation Ethics is not **FULLY** relativist: it has an absolute principle (love) that is non-negotiable.

FOUR WORKING PRINCIPLES

In Situation Ethics there are **FOUR WORKING PRINCIPLES** (Fletcher's own term)

1. **PRAGMATISM** - What you propose must be practical - work in practice.

2. **RELATIVISM** - There are no fixed, absolute rules - all decisions are relative to **AGAPE** love. If love demands that you steal food, then you should steal food.

3. **POSITIVISM** - Kant and Natural Law are based on reason as both theories argue reason can uncover the right course of action. Fletcher disagrees with this: you have to start with a **POSITIVE** choice or commitment - you need to want to do good. There is no rational answer to the question "why should I love?"

4. **PERSONALISM** - People come first: you cannot sacrifice people to rules or laws.

SIX FUNDAMENTAL PRINCIPLES

1. Nothing is good in itself except **LOVE** (it is the only thing that is absolutely good, the only thing with intrinsic value).

2. Jesus replaced the law with love or **AGAPE**. "The ruling norm of Christian decision is love, nothing else," Joseph Fletcher.

3. Love and **JUSTICE** are the same thing (if love is put into practice it can only result in fair treatment and fair distribution).

4. Love desires the good of **OTHERS** (it does not have favourites, but this doesn't mean we have to **LIKE** them).

5. Only the **END JUSTIFIES THE MEANS** (if an action causes harm, it is wrong. If good comes of it, it is right).

6. Love's decisions are made in each **SITUATION**.

STRENGTHS

- **RELATIVE** - As a relative ethical theory it is able to adjust the moral outcomes on the basis of the individual situation. This fits with the experience of world where no two situations are identical.

- **CHRISTIAN ETHICS** - Situation Ethics is the only truly Christian ethical theory because it is based on the teaching and example of Jesus' life. For example, in the parable of the **GOOD SAMARITAN** Jesus tells the teacher of the law to "go and do the loving thing."

- **MORAL RESPONSIBILITY** - Situation Ethics gives individuals moral responsibility. They choose the correct course of action by working it out and assessing the situation to determine the most loving course of action.

- **ETHIC FOR THE FUTURE** - Bishop Robinson described it as "an ethic for man coming of age" meaning that it can help people adapt and deal with new moral dilemmas that occur.

WEAKNESSES

- **DEMANDS OF LOVE** - Love is a very demanding value to place at the centre of your ethics - can anyone love sacrificially all the time? Mustn't we be selfish some of the time?

- **PREDICT THE FUTURE** - Like all **CONSEQUENTIALIST** theories it's impossible to calculate into the future making this particular love calculation **IMPOSSIBLE.**

- **VALUE OF LAW** - William Barclay argues that Fletcher fails to realise the value of law - as an expression of the collective wisdom of generations before us, so the moral law is a guide which we shouldn't throw away so easily. Law also defines the **FABRIC** of society.

- **NO CHRISTIAN SUPPORT** - Despite being designed as the new ethical theory, Situation Ethics has been rejected by a number of Christian Churches for being relative. **POPE PIUS XII** called it "an individualist and subjective appeal to the concrete circumstances of action to justify decisions in opposition to the **NATURAL LAW** or God's revealed will."

KEY QUOTES

1. *"Love alone is always good and right in every situation." Joseph Fletcher (1966:69)*

2. *"There can be and often is a conflict between law and love." Joseph Fletcher (1966:70)*

3. *"Too much law means the obliteration of the individual; too much individualism means a weakening of the law ... there is a place for law as the encourager of morality." William Barclay*

4. *"Love is the ultimate law because it is the negation of law; it is absolute because it concerns everything concrete." Paul Tillich*

5. *In 1952 POPE PIUS XII called situation ethics "an individualistic and subjective appeal to the concrete circumstances of actions to justify decisions in opposition to the NATURAL LAW or God's revealed will'.*

CONFUSIONS TO AVOID

1. "Situation Ethics is Christian relativism." This idea needs careful handling. In fact there is one non-negotiable absolute at the heart of Situation Ethics - agape (selfless, sacrificial) love. But this is a principle, not a rule. Therefore as it is applied, it is made relative to the most loving outcome. Fletcher himself describes Situation Ethics as "relativistic" as it "relativises the absolute, it does not absolutise the relative." Compare Fletcher with Pastor Dietrich Bonhoeffer who believed the most loving thing was to join the 1944 Stauffenberg bomb plot against Hitler (an action which cost him his life).

2. "Jesus was a situationist." Again, be careful about a bland statement to this effect. Jesus maintained he "came not to abolish the law, but to fulfil it," although a key part of his mission seemed to be to overthrow the old Jewish purity code (he didn't like stoning adulterers (see John 8), or treating unclean women as "impure and untouchable," (see Mark 5), both required by Leviticus 18-19). The young man of Mark 7 is commended for keeping the law but then invited to "give up all his possessions and come, follow me!" The nearest Jesus comes to situationism is in the discussion of the parable of the Good Samaritan, where the teacher of the law is invited to "go and do likewise" in each situation requiring agape love (Luke 10:29-37). Indeed, the parable is worth studying in the light of Fletcher's teaching. It's about the meaning and application of agape love.

ISSUES ARISING FROM SITUATION ETHICS

Exam Board Checklist AQA AS Unit A

1. Strengths and weaknesses of Situation Ethics as an ethical system

2. Does Christian love allow people to do anything, depending on the context, and how far is it true that love should be the highest Christian law, overruling all others when necessary?

3. How practical is Situation Ethics? Remember to apply to one ethical issue **APART FROM ABORTION AND EUTHANASIA**.

4. How compatible is Situation Ethics with other Christian approaches to moral decision-making?

GET MORE HELP

Get more help with situation ethics by using the links below:

http://i-pu.sh/G9T09F03

Religious Teaching on the Nature and Value of Human Life

For millennia human beings have sought answers to the key questions of existence. What does it mean to be human? Am I free to make my own decisions? How should I engage in a relationship with my fellow humans? Here we will explore these questions from the perspective of Christianity.

KEY TERMS

- **DETERMINISM** - The belief that all actions, including human ones, are determined by causes external to the will.

- **FATE** - The view that a person's life is controlled by a force (usually supernatural) outside of their control.

- **FREE WILL** - The power of action without constraint of necessity or fate.

- **AGAPE** - Christian love taught by Jesus that is selfless.

- **PREDESTINATION** - The belief that God has laid out all that will happen including the salvation of some humans.

- **HUMAN CONDITION** - The unique features and experiences of human beings.

- **ANTHROPOCENTRIC** - Regarding human beings as the most central or important beings on the planet.

WHAT DOES IT MEAN TO BE HUMAN FOR A CHRISTIAN?

For Christians the relationship between the individual and God is an essential part of what it means to be a human. Through **COMMUNION** with various prophets God has provided guidance for human action. This should be seen as a model for how humans should treat other human beings. In Exodus "the Ten Commandments" are provided by God as essential rules for life. Four of the rules govern the relationship between God and humanity, eg worship only one God, do not worship false idols, and keep the Sabbath holy. In addition, there are six rules which apply between individual humans, eg do not murder, steal or commit adultery.

Jesus clarified the importance of this relationship in his response to the Pharisee when he was asked "what is the greatest commandment?" Jesus replied "Love the Lord your God with all your heart and with all your soul and with all your mind and with all your strength." The second is this: 'Love your neighbour as yourself.' There is no commandment greater than these," (Mark 12:30:31). In the original text the Greek word **AGAPE** was used for love. The relationship between humans should therefore be one of **MUTUAL RESPECT** and **SELFLESSNESS**.

For many Christians Jesus, as the **INCARNATION** of God on Earth, represents the ideal perfection of human action. Jesus demonstrated what it meant to be human. These Christians consider the question 'What Would Jesus Do? (WWJD) when approaching a moral decision and use this as a guide. Jesus' teaching of **AGAPE** permeated all He did; therefore what it means to be human is to act with **RESPECT** and **SELFLESSNESS** for other people. Act of charity, kindness and generosity are ideal Christian perfections. In the 'Parable of the Sheep and the Goats' Jesus states "truly I tell you, whatever you did for one of the least of these brothers and sisters of mine, you did for me," (Matthew 25:40). This teaches that kind actions towards others will be rewarded with eternal life.

It is also expected that humans will show **HUMILITY** before God. This includes; having faith in God's existence and teachings, as well as, the importance of prayer for humans. Jesus enforced this when he said, "if you believe, you will receive whatever you ask for in prayer," (Matthew 21:22).

The faithfulness of the prophets, those blessed by God, is also repeatedly emphasised and tested. In "The Binding of Isaac" (Genesis 22) God asks Abraham to sacrifice his son Isaac as a test of **FAITH**. Abraham agrees and just before the final act God commands Abraham to stop and God provides lamb for sacrifice instead. In the book of Job, Satan under permission for God, tests the faith of Job by ruining his life, taking away all his possessions, and causing him physical harm. Job never gives up his faith or curses God and as a result he is returned to health and made twice as prosperous. In both of these examples the faithful are rewarded in life showing the power of faith for a human. "And without faith it is impossible to please God, because anyone who comes to him must believe that he exists and that he rewards those who earnestly seek him," (Hebrews 11:6).

The story of creation presents humans with a **UNIQUE** nature and purpose. This **SANCTITY OF LIFE** presents human life as sacred and holy and is a fundamental teaching of the Catholic Church. As humans were created in the **IMAGE OF GOD** their life has intrinsic worth. Furthermore, it is the act of creation that establishes this **SANCTITY**. God knows each individual thoroughly meaning they are equally valuable He states, "before I formed you in the womb I knew you, before you were born I set you apart; I appointed you as a prophet to the nations," (Jeremiah 1:5). Critically, this is an **ANTHROPOCENTRIC** view of life as it only applies to humans. Animals, although important to protect, can be used as a "means to an end" whilst humans must be treated as an "end in themselves."

Another important feature of human nature is the ability to make a **FREE CHOICE**. In Genesis, humans are created with **FREE WILL**. Unfortunately, unable to resist the temptation, Adam and Eve chose to **SIN**. This action brought suffering, pain and death into the world. The Catholic tradition, following the teaching of **AUGUSTINE**, claim this **ORIGINAL SIN** is "seminally" present in all humans meaning that **ALL** humans suffer as a result. God tests humans through challenges and their responses determine their fate.

For many Catholics, what it means to be human is to overcome the temptation of **SIN**. Through choosing correctly humans can avoid sin and secure eternal life with God. **AQUINAS** by claiming "man chooses not out of necessity but freely" asserted that humans are free **AUTONOMOUS** beings. Without this freedom would be impossible to join the divide between humans and God.

TO WHAT EXTENT ARE CHRISTIANS FREE?

For some Christians the view that humans have complete freedom is too much. Instead they claim that God has a **PLAN** for each individual. Passages in the Bible such as "For I know the plans I have for you," declares the Lord, "plans to prosper you and not to harm you, plans to give you hope and a future" (Jeremiah 29:11) and "In their hearts humans plan their course, but the Lord establishes their steps" (Proverbs 16:9) bolster this belief that God is watching over them and provides them with comfort through difficult periods in life. Crucially, this view of human nature does not remove free will entirely. An individual can choose **NOT** to follow God's plan for them but they will face the consequences.

PAUL'S claim, "Does not the potter have the right to make out of the same lump of clay some pottery for special purposes and some for common use?" (Romans 9:21) has for many people stood in opposition of free will.

JOHN CALVIN, following **PAUL** argued for a **FATALISTIC** view of human nature. He asserted that before the Creation, God determined the **FATE** of the universe throughout all of time and space. This included the moral actions of all humans. "God preordained ... a part of the human race, without any merit of their own, to eternal salvation, and another part, in just punishment of their sin, to eternal damnation."

Calvin justified this as a result of God **OMNISCIENCE**. At the moment of creation He already knew who was going to heaven. These Calvin called the **ELECTED**. All future events including human choices are predestined to happen because God knew they were going to happen. If the future was uncertain then God would not be omniscient.

This view has a number of conclusions. Humans have no **MORAL CHOICE** and their salvation is predetermined by God, not by the actions of humans themselves. Sin is also irreversible and humans have no ability to change their **FATE**. If they are part of the **ELECTED** then they will be saved. If they are not they will be **DAMNED**. This is a brute fact of the universe and a necessity derived from Gods qualities. God "guides whom he will and leads astray whom he will," (Calvin).

CALVIN claimed **PAUL'S** scripture justified this, "for those God foreknew he also predestined to be conformed to the image of his Son, that he might be the firstborn among many brothers and sisters. And those he predestined, he also called; those he called, he also justified; those he justified, he also glorified," (Romans 8:29-30).

HOW SHOULD CHRISTIANS TREAT OTHER HUMANS?

Race

Both the modern and traditional Christian values stand, on the whole, in opposition to **RACISM**. There are a number of justifications for this.

In the beginning "God created mankind in his own image, in the image of God he created them; male and female he created them" (Genesis 1:27). All humans, regardless of ethnicity, deserve the same **RESPECT** and **DIGNITY** and should be treated with **EQUALITY**. Prejudice and discrimination is violating the **UNION** that humans share with God and is wrong. **PAUL** took this further when he said "From one man he made all the nations, that they should inhabit the whole earth; and he marked out their appointed times in history and the boundaries of their lands," (Acts 17:26). God has established all the people of the earth and they are part of same act of creation.

Others turn to Jesus for guidance. The meaning of "to love your neighbour" was clarified by Jesus in the parable of the **GOOD SAMARITAN**. Here he shows that every human is your **NEIGHBOUR** regardless of any difference and that it is the DUTY of anybody to help another in need. There should be no discrimination of individuals as all humans are equal before God.

PAUL further opposes prejudice and discrimination. In his letter to the Corinthians he wrote "There is neither Jew nor Greek, neither slave nor free, nor is there male and female, for you are all one in Christ Jesus," (Galatians 3:28). Here **PAUL** is claiming that there is no difference between Christians. All are equal in the eyes of God and their individual **DIGNITY** should be protected.

Despite these teachings there are a minority who use the Bible of justification for discrimination on the basis of race. Some interpretations of the "Curse of Ham" state that Noah cursed his son Ham with "black skin." This curse has been used as justification for **OPPRESSION** of the Canaans by the Israelites but also for the denigration of black people. In addition to the "curse of Ham" the Old Testament justifies the practise of **SLAVERY** in certain circumstances. The books of **EXODUS**, **LEVITICUS** and **DEUTERONOMY** set out these criteria including; debt bondage, sexual slavery, and the trading of slaves.

Critically, although present in the Bible, these views are held to be outdated cultural practises that have been superseded by later teachings and are no longer applicable in the debate on **RACISM**.

Gender

There is less consistency over gender issues that there is to race within Christianity. Many are of the opinion that men are women are **EQUAL** in the **EYES OF GOD**. They use the same justification outlined above; "you should love your neighbour as yourself," humans are made in the "image of God," and "there is neither Jew nor Greek" to support the equality of women. Others point to the significance of the Virgin Mary in Catholicism and Jesus' fair treatment of women to justify equality and the importance women in society.

However, others feel that women should have different **ROLES** within society. Within Catholicism women can be neither priests nor bishops, whilst the Church of England vote on women bishops in 2012 was rejected.

Some use the example of Jesus as support for the different roles of women in society. In the Bible, Jesus appointed 12 **MALE** apostles. These men were given the role of spreading the gospel. The **PATRIACHAL** headship of the Church represents this tradition of male leadership and should be retained within the Church.

The letters of **PAUL** provide further scripture supporting the differing role of women. He writes: "Women should remain silent in the churches. They are not allowed to speak, but must be in submission, as the Law says. If they want to enquire about something, they should ask their own husbands at home; for it is disgraceful for a woman to speak in the church," (1 Corinthians 14:34-35) and highlighted the supremacy of men when he states:"Now I want you to realise that the head of every man is Christ, and the head of the woman is man, and the head of Christ is God." (1 Corinthians 11:3)

Disability

Historically disability has been associated with a "curse" from God or punishment for sin. God outlines the punishment for disobedience when He states "I will bring on you sudden terror, wasting diseases and fever that will destroy your sight and sap your strength," (Leviticus 26:16). In addition, God punishes Miriam with leprosy for disbelief in Moses; the Egyptians are punished with sickness and plagues for refusal to follow instructions, whilst King David's illegitimate child with Bathsheba died of a sickness as punishment for their sin.

In the Old Testament suffering can also be seen as a **TEST OF FAITH**. That many people receive challenges in their life which, as part of God's plan, is aimed at strengthening their belief. The book of Job outlines the rewards for an individual for surviving these tests of life. "Consider what God has done: Who can straighten what he has made crooked?" (Ecclesiastes 7:13)

SIN also has lasting consequences that can affect subsequent generations. In Genesis God punishes both Adam and Cain for their disobedience. The impact of this sin causes continual hardship for their kin. God tells Moses "I, the Lord your God, am a jealous God, punishing the children for the sin of the parents to the third and fourth generation of those who hate me," (Exodus 20:5) indicating that the suffering of a child could be the result of sin by the family.

The example of Jesus in the Bible has also given people a model for how to act towards disability. Jesus performed healing **MIRACLES** on lepers, the deaf, physically disabled and the sick. Most understood this teaching as an instruction to Christians to act with **COMPASSION** and **KINDNESS** towards people with disability, however, understood differently it can be seen as an invitation to **FAITH**. That through belief in Jesus you can achieve **SALVATION** from suffering and the resurrection of a body made perfect in eternal life.

After the death of Christ, suffering of an individual was associated with **REDEMPTION**. If we suffer in our daily lives we can connect to the suffering of Christ. **PAUL** writes "Now I rejoice in what I am suffering for you, and I fill up in my flesh what is still lacking in regard to Christ's afflictions, for the sake of his body, which is the church. (Colossians 1:24).

In the 20th Century, as the cultural understanding towards disability changed so did the Christian attitude. Both the Catholic and Anglican Churches now emphasis the importance of **COMPASSION** and care towards those with disability. This is now the majority attitude. They believe that the following teachings supersede any negative attitude towards disability:

- Jesus performed healing miracles teaching Christians to act with compassion towards the sick

- In the parable of the Sheep and the Goats Jesus instructs Christians to help the needy.

- The parable of the Good Samaritan teaches that there should be no discrimination between individuals

- The teaching of loving your neighbour shows that compassion and love should be shown to all people

- The belief that humans are made in the 'image of God' means that all people regardless of disability share in the sanctity of life and dignity of the individual

These teachings focus on the **EQUALITY** of all humans and the **DUTY** of everyone to treat others with **RESPECT** and **DIGNITY**.

WHAT IS THE VALUE OF HUMAN LIFE?

For Christians human life is **INTRINSICALLY** valuable. They have been given a **SOUL** by God that makes them unique. Animals although valuable **DO NOT** have a soul. The human soul is **IMMORTAL** and not of this earth. It was created out of the divine breath that God breathed into Adam in the moment of creation.

> "Then the Lord God formed a man from the dust of the ground and breathed into his nostrils the breath of life, and the man became a living being." (Genesis 2:7)

In this act of creation God set humans aside from the rest of creation. He commands Adam and Eve to "Be fruitful and increase in number; fill the earth and subdue it. Rule over the fish in the sea and the birds in the sky and over every living creature that moves on the ground." (Genesis 1:28) Humans are assigned **STEWARDSHIP** of the planet. They have control over the created Earth but must act responsibly towards it and animals.

AUGUSTINE believed that humans were different from other animals due to their **RATIONALITY**. He writes "Man, then ... is a rational soul with a mortal and earthly body in its service." Consciousness and the human ability to think are distinguishing features of humanity and make them more important than animals. This rationality does not come without cost. He claims "what made Adam capable of obeying God's commands also made him able to sin." Thus, free will can result in sin.

This intrinsic value of human life s is a key feature of Catholic thought. It is the motivating reason for rejecting abortion, euthanasia and other ethical issues that involve the destruction of actual or potential life.

IS SOME LIFE MORE VALUABLE THAN OTHERS?

Some believe that for God some life is more valuable than others. Sinners are less valuable. On judgement day, all humans will be **JUDGED**. Those who have not followed the commandments of God will receive punishment. **CALVIN** as we saw earlier claimed that this decision was made before the beginning of the world, whilst, others think that true **REPENTANCE** for sins will result in **FORGIVENESS**.

> *"If we confess our sins, he is faithful and just and will forgive us our sins and purify us from all unrighteousness." (1 John 1:9)*

Many believe that value is achieved through **SERVICE** and dedication to God. It is for this reason that they might join the monastic orders. This **DUTY** they feel is what it means to be a true Christian. A life of service entails **SELF SACRIFICE**. Monks and nuns abstain from sex and other worldly temptations to gain **UNION** with God and cleanse themselves of sin. Others dedicate their lives to supporting and helping others as part of their **MORAL DUTY**.

The ultimate act of **SELF SACRIFICE** would be to give up your own life. This mirrors the act of sacrifice by Jesus on the cross where He surrendered to the will of God for the love of **HUMANITY**. Such actions by humans are held with high regard and many martyrs have been canonised as saints. Importantly, self sacrifice is not suicide. The distinguishing feature is the **INTENT** of the individual. True self sacrifice is the **SELFLESS** intent is to save another person whereas in suicide the intention is the **SELFISH** desire of death. Those who give up their lives for others truly embody the teaching of **PAUL** when he said "you were bought at a price. Therefore honour God with your bodies," (1 Corinthians 6:20).

HUMAN LIFE OVER ANIMAL LIFE

The **ANTHROPOCENTRIC** nature of Christianity has already been outlined. However, this is not the view of all Christians. Although generally accepted to be second to human life animal life is believed to have moral worth for the following reasons:

- Animals are part of the created world and deserve respect.

- Animals play and important role in the lives of St Antony of Padua, St Brigit, St Columba and St Brendan.

- St Francis of Assisi said "If you have men who will exclude any of God's creatures from the shelter of compassion and pity, you will have men who will deal likewise with their fellow men."

- God is an immanent God. He cares for all creation.

- The Bible teaches the importance of responsibility. Looking after animals is the most responsible thing to do.

- The example of God as a loving God shows humans they should be compassionate towards animals.

- Jesus taught that Christians should protect the weak.

- Agape is selfless and non-preferential. It also does not require you are loved back. To show love without compensation is the best action you can take.

KEY QUOTES

1. *If we confess our sins, he is faithful and just and will forgive us our sins and purify us from all unrighteousness." (1 John 1:9)*

2. *"Man, then ... is a rational soul with a mortal and earthly body in its service." (Augustine)*

3. *"Love the Lord your God with all your heart and with all your soul and with all your mind and with all your strength.' The second is this: 'Love your neighbour as yourself.' There is no commandment greater than these." (Mark 12:30:31)*

4. *"Does not the potter have the right to make out of the same lump of clay some pottery for special purposes and some for common use?" (Romans 9:21)*

5. *"Consider what God has done: Who can straighten what he has made crooked?" (Ecclesiastes 7:13)*

6. *"There is neither Jew nor Greek, neither slave nor free, nor is there male and female, for you are all one in Christ Jesus." (Galatians 3:28)*

CONFUSIONS TO AVOID

1. Be clear to identify arguments against race and disability equality as a **MINORITY** opinion. Few people today use the Bible to justify racism or to claim that disability is the result of sin.

2. Avoid using non-religious or secular answers in this section. The unit focuses on the religious view towards human life therefore you should learn specific answers coupled with evidence to sustain your points and avoid your essay becoming too generalised.

3. Be specific in your distinction between key terms. Candidates often confuse "human" and "non-human life." Describing embryos as "non-human" is risky because embryos are often included within the religious interpretation of life. Secondly, the distinction between "nature" and "value" of human life is important. The "nature" of human life refers to the experience of being human whereas "value" of human life questions if some types of life have more value than others.

RELIGIOUS TEACHING ON HUMAN LIFE

Exam Board Checklist AQA AS Unit A

1. How far must a religious view of life be fatalistic?

2. How far can religion support the idea of equality?

3. "Human life must be given priority over non-human life and some human lives are more valuable than others" - how far could religion accept this view?

GET MORE HELP

Get more help with the nature and value of human life by using the links below:

http://i-pu.sh/Z0W42C63

Abortion

SOME DEFINITIONS

ABORTION can be natural (miscarriage) or by medical procedure (using drugs or killing and dismembering a foetus). A **FOETUS** exists from 8eight weeks onwards, when the embryo assumes the basic shape of the newborn and all the organs are present; an **EMBRYO** from conception to eight weeks. **PRE-EMBRYO** is now being used to denote the collection of cells up to 14 days old, before the **PRIMITIVE STREAK** emerges (the faint streak which is the earliest trace of the embryo in the fertilized ovum).

LEGAL POSITION (UK)

The **1967 ABORTION ACT** legalised abortion up to 28 weeks with two doctor's consent a. for medical reasons b. for psychological reasons c. for family reasons d. in cases of disability. The legal term was changed in 1990 to 24 weeks. The age of **VIABILITY** (survivability) has now dropped to 22 weeks with medical advances. 85% of abortions occur under 18 weeks and there are around 200,000 abortions a year in the UK, representing 25% of pregnancies. Note: we do not have "abortion on demand" in the UK as the consent of two doctors is needed.

SANCTITY OF LIFE

- **SANCTITY OF LIFE** (sacredness) - biblical view **GENESIS 1:27**, we are made in the image of God, and "he knit you together in your mother's womb," **PSALM 139:6**. Human life has **INTRINSIC VALUE** because God himself "became flesh and lived among us" (**JOHN 1:14**). We are not our own, but we belong to God and our life is "on loan" from God. God appoints the day of our death "the Lord gave and the Lord takes away" **JOB 1:21**. "Do not murder" is a fundamental law, **EXODUS 20:13**, implying respect for all human life, and to the Catholic Church this includes embryonic life.

- **SANCTITY OF LIFE** - the Natural Law view. **EVANGELIUM VITAE** (1995 Papal encyclical) argues society has undermined the sanctity of life and produced a "culture of death" in its attitude to foetal life, the elderly and the handicapped. So "every person open to truth can recognise the sacred value of human life from its beginning to its end" - as St. Paul notes "even Gentiles have the law written on their hearts," (**ROMANS 2:14-15**). Abortion breaks two **PRIMARY PRECEPTS** of reproduction and preservation of life - as human life begins at conception. We know this through Aquinas' **SYNDERESIS** principle: innately we "do good and avoid evil" in line with our rational purposes given by our human nature.

- **SANCTITY OF LIFE** - weak view. Some prefer the more universal, weaker idea of **RESPECT** for life. As medical science advances we know more eg about disabilities of foetuses or inherited diseases. **SITUATION ETHICS** sees **AGAPE** as a universal good, so the person's situation needs to be paramount, and **STANLEY HAUERWAS** argues that the Church has permitted the taking of life in the past eg when it is in the interests of others, or in cases of martyrdom.

QUALITY OF LIFE

Peter Singer maintains we would always choose a healthy child over a handicapped one. So "if aborting the abnormal foetus can be followed by having a normal one, it would be wrong not to do this." Note the usual consequentialist problem: how do we know? There is also the question of resources: how much does the handicapped child cost over its life relative to the healthy one? A utilitarian might argue the resources are better spent elsewhere. Is it the most loving outcome (Situation Ethics) to bring a suffering child into the world? Singer employs the **REPLACEMENT** argument - it is always better to replace a less happy child by a happier one - but does this justify **INFANTICIDE** - the killing of less healthy children? Or (as used to happen in Britain in the days of your family doctor) the smothering of abnormal infants?

HUMAN RIGHTS

Some argue that because the foetus shares the attributes of a person it should have full human rights (including the right to life). The logic of the argument from human rights is given below (P = proposition).

- **P1** - The unborn child is a human life (Is it? Even as a collection of cells?).

- **P2** - It is always wrong to take innocent human life.

- **P3** - Abortion involves the taking of innocent life.

- **P4** - Therefore abortion is wrong.

Notice that the meaning of "human life" has changed from "biological life" to something close to "personhood." The meaning has changed from P1 to P2 - note also the addition of the moral word "innocent."

WOMEN'S RIGHTS

JUDITH JARVIS THOMPSON employs the analogy of the violinist - after his friends kidnap you, you wake up plugged into a sick violinist who needs your kidneys. To unplug the violinist will kill him. It's only for nine months. Do you have the **RIGHT** to unplug the violinist? Does your right to choose what to do with your body outweigh the right to life? (Note the problems with this analogy - for example, pregnant women are not immobile, they are not kidnapped but choose to have sex, the foetus is arguably not actually a person). Thompson argues that to be forced to remain with a dependent being attached to you is **OUTRAGEOUS**.

PERSONHOOD

MARY ANNE WARREN asks "what characteristics make a person?" She lists: consciousness, reason, self-motivated activity, communication, self-awareness. "Genetic humanity is not enough" - we must have at least one of these criteria. "A foetus is a human being which is not yet a person, so cannot have full moral rights," argues Mary Anne Warren. Note: if you apply her criteria this would allow you to justify the killing of infants, coma victims and people asleep. **SINGER** agrees with **TOOLEY** who declared a human being "possesses a serious right to life only if it possesses the concept of a self as a continuing **SUBJECT OF EXPERIENCES** and other mental states, and believes that it is itself such a continuing entity." Infants do not qualify. In 1979 **SINGER** wrote, "Human babies are not born self-aware, or capable of grasping that they exist over time. They are not **PERSONS**," therefore, "the life of a newborn is of less value than the life of a pig, a dog, or a chimpanzee."

WHEN DOES LIFE BEGIN?

CASTI CONNUBII (1930, Papal encyclical) - persons at conception. **RC CATECHISM** "from the first moment of his existence a human being must be recognised as having the rights of a person - among which is the inviolable right of every innocent being to life." The **PRIMITIVE STREAK** is the first recognisable feature at 15 days. **QUICKENING** (movement) occurs at 100 days (approximately 14 weeks). Some time between 18 and 24 weeks the foetus feels pain. **VIABLILTY** (survivability out of the womb) exists around 22 weeks - but probability of survival is low. **MARY ANNE WARREN** sees birth as only morally relevant point as "the extension of equal moral status to foetuses threatens women's most basic rights. Unlike foetuses, women are already persons." **JONATHAN GLOVER** argues it is a matter of degree - a foetus is more of a person than an embryo, a baby is more than a foetus. Ultimately this is a **METAPHYSICAL** question to do with beliefs rather than science. **DON MARQUIS** argued that abortion is wrong because it deprives someone of a future and "the ethics of killing is self-evident" (but how do we know the future? What of the mother's future? How do we weigh the interests of a mother against a child?).

CHRISTIANS AND ABORTION

There is not one Christian view. The conservative view held by many Catholics and evangelicals holds that life is sacred from the point of conception because God the creator is behind and within this creation (Psalm 139 "God knit you together in your mother's womb"). Catholics follow a **NATURAL LAW** argument, pointing to the **PRIMARY PRECEPT** of preserving innocent life, and the **DIVINE LAW** "do not murder," whereas evangelicals appeal only to **SCRIPTURE**, a Divine Command Theory, eg **PSALM 139** (above). Liberal Christians might take a **SITUATION ETHICS** view of abortion, arguing that **AGAPE** (sacrificial) love is best maximised by considering the **PERSON** (but which person? Mother? Child?) and **OUTCOMES** (but how do we know?). Questions of **PERSONHOOD** are logically prior to any other judgement.

UTILITARIANS (UNIT A)

UTILITARIANS seek to do an empirical calculation of good over evil (or pleasure/pain). **HEDONIC** utilitarians like Bentham balance pleasure/pain (eg emotional, financial, personal pleasure/pain). **RULE** utilitarians (Mill) calculate from past experience what social rules maximise happiness (eg the misery/death caused by backstreet abortions vs happiness/misery of mothers having abortions). Rule utilitarians stress importance of **RIGHTS** and **JUSTICE**, but again, the question of whether the foetus is a person comes before we decide whether the mother's rights come before foetal rights. **PREFERENCE** utilitarians like **SINGER** might put more weight on a potential child's preferences, but in fact Singer's view of personhood (rational self-consciousness) allows for **INFANTICIDE** of disabled children.

ISSUES ARISING FROM ABORTION

Exam Board Checklist AQA AS Unit A

1. Does the definition of human life stop abortion being murder?

2. Can abortion and euthanasia ever be said to be 'good'?

3. Do humans have a right to life, and a right to choose to die?

GET MORE HELP

Get more help with abortion by using the links below:

http://i-pu.sh/K6G89P41

Euthanasia

DEFINITIONS

- **EUTHANASIA** (Greek = good death) is the practice of ending life to reduce pain and suffering (so "mercy killing").

- **VOLUNTARY** euthanasia = when a patient's death is caused by another person eg doctor with the **EXPLICIT CONSENT** of the patient. The patient request must be **VOLUNTARY** (acting without coercion, pressure), **ENDURING** (lasts some time or is repeated over time) and **COMPETENT** (they have the mental capacity to choose). A variation on euthanasia is **PHYSICIAN-ASSISTED SUICIDE** - this differs from euthanasia as the doctor will help the patient to commit suicide (eg set up the apparatus), but the final act of killing is done by the patient.

- **NON-VOLUNTARY** euthanasia is done **WITHOUT** the patient's consent, because they are not competent or able to give the consent (eg in a coma, on a life support machine). The doctor and/or the family may take the decision.

- **INVOLUNTARY** euthanasia is performed **AGAINST** the wishes of the patient. This is widely opposed and illegal in the UK as are all forms of assisted suicide and euthanasia.

ACTIVE OR PASSIVE

- **ACTIVE** euthanasia is the **DIRECT** and **DELIBERATE** killing of a patient.

- **PASSIVE** euthanasia is when life-sustaining treatment is withdrawn or withheld.

This distinction may also be described as the difference between an **ACT** and an **OMISSION** (failing to act) and between **KILLING** and **ALLOWING TO DIE**. Some, such as **JAMES RACHELS**, argue there is no real difference - if anything passive euthanasia (withdrawal of treatment) is worse because it leads to a longer, drawn out death and so more suffering potentially. **DAME CICELY SAUNDERS** (who founded the hospice movement) argues that it is unnecessary for anyone to suffer a painful death with modern drugs. A counter-argument is that many doctors already hasten death (eg by doubling a morphine dose): under the doctrine of **DOUBLE EFFECT** if the intention is to alleviate pain and a secondary effect to kill someone, the doctor is not guilty of any crime.

LEGAL POSITION

Until 1961 suicide was illegal in the UK. The **1961 SUICIDE ACT** legalised suicide but made it illegal to assist.

The **NETHERLANDS** and **SWITZERLAND** allow voluntary euthanasia (active and passive) and physician-assisted suicide. The **DIGNITAS** clinic in Switzerland helped 107 British people to die in 2010. **DR ANNE TURNER** (aged 66) was one such person in 2009 - subject of the docu-drama "A Short Stay in Switzerland." No-one has ever been prosecuted in the UK for helping a relative or friend go to Switzerland.

In 2010 Director of Public Prosecutions **KEIR STARMER** confirmed that relatives of people who kill themselves will not face prosecution as long as they do not maliciously encourage them and assist only a "clear settled and informed wish" to commit suicide. The move came after the Law Lords backed multiple sclerosis sufferer Debbie Purdy's call for a policy statement on whether people who help someone commit suicide should be prosecuted. In August 2012 Tony Nicklinson, with "locked-in syndrome," failed in his legal attempt to end his "intolerable life.".

Keir Starmer concluded: "There are **NO GUARANTEES** against prosecution and it is my job to ensure that the most vulnerable people are protected while at the same time giving enough information to those people like Mrs Purdy who want to be able to make informed decisions about what actions they may choose to take."

The **OREGON RULES** are another attempt to legalise assisted suicide by laying down conditions under which it will be allowed in US law.

SANCTITY OF LIFE - BIBLE

The Bible argues that life is a gift from God. Humans are created in the **IMAGE OF GOD** (Genesis 1:27) and the **INCARNATION** (God taking human form - John 1:14) shows the sacred value of human life. Human life is a **GIFT** or **LOAN** from God "The Lord gave and the Lord has taken away," (Job 1:21). We should also show **RESPECT** for human life: "thou shalt not murder," (Exodus 20:13). We should also "choose life" (Deuteronomy 30). Finally, Christian love (**AGAPE**) is crucial "the greatest value of all is love" (1 Corinthians 13). We should protect human life (the parable of the Good Samaritan) particularly as God gave his only son to redeem us (bring us back from sin and death) and give us the gift of "life in all its fullness."

SANCTITY OF LIFE - NATURAL LAW

The **NATURAL LAW** view argues that there is a **PRIMARY PRECEPT** to "preserve life" and views life as an **INTRINSIC** good. Euthanasia is therefore wrong and the Catholic Church forbids both active and passive euthanasia as "contrary to the dignity of the human person and the respect due to God, his creator" (Catechism of the Roman Catholic Church). However, the **DOCTRINE OF DOUBLE EFFECT** might accept the shortening of human life (eg if the intention is to relieve pain, secondary effect to kill) so long as it is only a **FORESEEN BUT UNINTENDED RESULT**. The Catholic Church also makes a distinction between **ORDINARY** means (ordinary, usual medical treatments) and **EXTRAORDINARY** means (treatments that are dangerous, a huge burden, or disproportionate). It is morally acceptable to stop extraordinary means, as "it is the refusal of over-zealous treatment."

> *"Discontinuing medical procedures that are burdensome, dangerous, extraordinary, or disproportionate to the expected outcome can be legitimate; it is the refusal of "over-zealous" treatment. Here one does not will to cause death; one's inability to impede it is merely accepted. The decisions should be made by the patient if he is competent and able or, if not, by those legally entitled to act for the patient, whose reasonable will and legitimate interests must always be respected." RC Catechism 2278*

QUALITY OF LIFE

JAMES RACHELS argues that the sanctity of life tradition places too much value on human life and there are times (eg with abortion and euthanasia) when this is unhelpful. He makes a distinction between **BIOLOGICAL LIFE** ("being alive" = functioning biological organism) and **BIOGRAPHICAL LIFE** ("having a life" = everything that makes us who we are). He says that what matters is biographical life and if this is already over (for example in a **PERSISTENT VEGETATIVE STATE or PVS**), then taking away biological life is acceptable.

PETER SINGER argues that the worth of human life varies (the value of human life is not a sacred gift but depends on its **QUALITY**). A low quality of life (judged by the patient) can justify them taking their life or justify someone else doing it for them.

AUTONOMY

JOHN STUART MILL (On Liberty, 1859) argues that individuals should have full **AUTONOMY** (the freedom to make decisions without coercion) so long as it does not harm other people. Individuals cannot be compelled to do things for their own good - "over his own mind-body the individual is sovereign." Those who support voluntary euthanasia believe that personal autonomy and self-determination (choosing what happens to you) are crucial. Any competent adult should be able to decide on the time and manner of their death.

KANT assumes autonomy as one of his three key postulates (with God and immortality). We are self-legislating, free moral beings. However, he argued in an essay on suicide that suicide was self-contradictory as, if it was universalised, the human race would die out.

WEAKNESSES

- **PALLIATIVE CARE** - Dame Cicely Saunders argues that there is a better alternative for euthanasia in providing a pain-free death for terminally ill patients. The **HOSPICE** movement may be seen as an alternative, **BUT**, the euthanasia supporter might argue, this level of care is not available to everyone, is expensive and cannot fully relieve a patient's suffering (eg for someone who cannot breathe unassisted).

- **VOLUNTARY AND COMPETENT** - Some raise questions about voluntary euthanasia. Can the patient ever be free from coercion (eg relatives who want an inheritance or doctors who need to free up resources)? Is the patient likely to be competent (eg when under high doses of medication, or when depressed, or senile). Response would be that there are at least some clear cases when patients **ARE** clearly voluntary (not coerced) and competent. Guidelines such as Starmer's or the **OREGON RULES** require a certain time period of repeated requests to different people, which are then independently confirmed.

- **SLIPPERY SLOPE** - This is the argument that once allowed, the outcome will be a process of a further decline in respect for human life and will end with the practice of non-voluntary euthanasia for the elderly seen as "unaffordable" by the working majority. A response might be that there is a clear difference between voluntary and non-voluntary euthanasia. Is there any evidence of a slippery slope in the state of Oregon or Switzerland? The rules on assisted suicide are drawn up precisely to stop the slide into widespread disrespect for human life.

- **DOCTOR-PATIENT RELATIONSHIP** - Some argue that doctors have a duty to preserve life (the **HIPPOCRATIC OATH**). Euthanasia will undermine the trust between patient and doctor if there is a fear that they will seek to end their life. However, as with abortion, there will remain doctors opposed to euthanasia which a patient could always choose, and it is highly unlikely that GPs will have any say in the process of mercy killing.

GET MORE HELP

Get more help with euthanasia by using the links below:

http://i-pu.sh/N5T15S95

Genetic Engineering (optional)

Note: this is an example of an ethical issue that you could choose. If you have chosen another issue, please ignore this section. You are required by the syllabus to add **ONE** issue of your own choice to the required areas of **ABORTION** and **EUTHANASIA**.

Genetic Engineering (**GE**) involves the practice of changing the genetic makeup of plants, animals or humans, or taking recombinant **DNA** (hybrid **DNA** made by artificially joining pieces of DNA from different sources) and using it for a special purpose. Novel reproductive technologies, such as those used in the cloning of sheep like Dolly, do not technically involve **GE**.

A **GENE** is a sequence of **DNA** made up of just four chemical letters. There are approximately 24,000 genes in the human body. If all the **DNA** in all the cells in one person were stretched out they would reach to the moon and back 8,000 times. 20% of our genes are now **PATENTED** by those who discovered them. Similarly **GM SEED** is owned by the seed company that engineered it - and cannot be sown without their permission (or purchase).

ISSUES

1. For what **PURPOSE** (making money? choosing eye colour? eliminating disease?).

2. With what **CONSEQUENCES** for biodiversity (plants) or human flourishing (**EUDAIMONIA**)?

3. Who decides? Do we as parents have the **RIGHT TO A CHILD** who is disease free? Is this an individual or social issue?

4. Should we **PLAY GOD** and manipulate nature?

5. Will a **SLIPPERY SLOPE** develop where one change leads to further unanticipated bad effects - such as the lowering of value of those with disabilities?

PRESENT POSITION

The **GENOME** was fully sequenced by Craig Ventner by 2003 . Now it is possible to screen for genetic defects (**PRENATAL GENETIC DIAGNOSIS - PGD**) as part of IVF treatment, alter genetic makeup **IN UTERO** (in the uterus) and create **GENE THERAPIES** from **STEM CELLS** for potential treatment of various diseases. **DOLLY** the sheep was cloned in 1996 and had three parent sheep - one provided the egg, one the DNA and one the womb (though the South Korean scientist who claimed to have cloned humans proved to be a fraud). **CROPS** have been genetically modified by companies like **MONSANTO**.

THE LAW

The **HUMAN FERTILITY AND EMBRYOLOGY ACT** (2008) established an authority for regulating genetic engineering in humans (the **HFEA**). **CLONING** is illegal unless a special **LICENCE** is obtained (first granted in 2004). Human and animal gametes (two cells fused during fertilisation) can also be mixed (**NEWCASTLE UNIVERSITY**, 2006). **GENETIC ENGINEERING** of embryos is not allowed in order to prevent a disability/ genetically inherited disease: you can select embryos for desirable genes and three person IVF treatment has just been legalised (2013) to prevent mitochondrial disease. **MULTIPLE** embryos can be fertilised - with issues of embryo wastage as the **BEST** are selected (shades of the wise men of Sparta selecting which baby lived or died). Or sperm can be injected directly into one egg - which most Christians find perfectly morally acceptable as no **WASTAGE** of embryos occurs. In the UK you can only select embryos for desirable genes- to create **SAVIOUR SIBLINGS** as in the film **MY SISTER'S KEEPER**.

UNNATURAL

Natural Law theory suggests we should not change the inviolable ousia (essence) or telos (goal) of any living organism. Both concepts come directly from Aristotelian philosophy. The GE of female turkeys to make them less broody (so that they lay more eggs), has been attacked by Jeremy **RIFKIN** as 'a serious violation of the intrinsic value of the creature'. RC Church argues that "a strictly therapeutic intervention whose explicit objective is the healing of various maladies such as those stemming from chromosomal defects will, in principle, be considered **DESIRABLE**, provided it is directed to the true promotion of the personal well-being of the individual without doing harm to his integrity or worsening his conditions of life." (Donum Vitae). But **CLONING** is absolutely prohibited, and embryo **WASTAGE** considered as evil as **ABORTION** - an assault on the **SANCTITY OF LIFE**.

PLAYING GOD

Is GE good **STEWARDSHIP** or evil **DOMINION** (Genesis 1:26)? One-third of all agricultural production world-wide is lost to pests and diseases, and there is enormous scope for GE to render crops resistant to pests, drought and frost, to improve yields and to enable food to be produced in harsh environments. Some Christians argue we should use the new technology to feed a hungry world and to distribute its benefits more equitably. Others fear the consequences of upsetting biodiversity or exploiting poor farmers who are buying seed that they cannot resow next year. There is a evidence of a rise in suicide rates among Indian farmers who have been sold patented GM seed - is there a link?

CONSEQUENCES

There are 5,000 inherited diseases (such as sickle cell anaemia) which could be eliminated with mass genetic screening. Is this not a moral **GOOD**? Others argue that the **SANCTITY OF HUMAN LIFE** is violated and there will be **SOCIAL CONSEQUENCES** such as the change in perception about human suffering or the creation of a super-race (with two tiers of society like in the film **GATTACA**). To eliminate imperfections is to change the idea of being human, bowing to the **UTILITARIAN** argument that anything that produces human suffering is wrong, which many Christians reject due to the **REDEMPTIVE SUFFERING** of Jesus on the Cross.

RIGHTS

Do I have the **RIGHT TO CHOOSE** the genetic makeup of a child? Or to have specially designed child to save another? Do I have a **DUTY** not to bring into the world a child who will suffer (perhaps in the same way as I did as a person with a genetic disease?)? Does a child have the **RIGHT TO KNOW** who are their genetic parents? Since 2005 the answer is "yes" - and sperm donor fathers have declined rapidly. Who has the right over a **SURROGATE** baby? Suppose the mother changes her mind? In America a famous case, the case of **BABY M**, involved a surrogate mother who changed her mind and refused to hand the baby over. The Catholic Church approves **GENETIC THERAPY** but disapproves strongly of **GENETIC ENHANCEMENT** where a child's characteristics are improved .

> "The production of human beings selected according to sex or other predetermined qualities, which change the genotype of the individual and of the human species, are contrary to the PERSONAL DIGNITY of the human being, to his integrity and to his identity. Therefore they can be in no way justified on the pretext that they will produce some beneficial results for humanity." Donum Vitae, Roman Catholic encyclical

Many people argue that GE opens a new era of **EUGENICS** so discredited by Nazi ideology, where genetic breeding is used to create a super-race.

GET MORE HELP

Get more help with genetic engineering by using the links below:

http://i-pu.sh/V5B08C26

The Four Questions Answered

The first section of this book mentioned that there are four questions we need to ask of any moral theory. They spell the acronym **DARM** (**D**erivation, **A**pplication, **R**ealism, **M**otivation).

1. HOW IS THE IDEA OF GOODNESS DERIVED?

Goodness has to come from somewhere - it is, after all a human construct. The normal candidates are three:

1. God
2. Reason
3. Observation or experience.

RELATIVISTS argue that our idea of goodness comes directly from **CULTURE** (what JL Mackie in Inventing Right and Wrong calls "forms of life") or from **EXPERIENCE** (the utilitarian or situationist view that we judge right and wrong according to circumstances and likely consequences).

UTLITARIANS see goodness as a **TELEOLOGICAL** idea depending on the end we pursue, either **PLEASURE** (the psychological "sovereign two masters, pleasure and pain" of Bentham) or **HAPPINESS** (it is good because most people desire it as an end in itself, says **MILL**). So goodness is measurable, an **OBJECTIVE, EMPIRICAL IDEA**, either by counting **HEDONS** (Bentham) or **DESIRES** (Mill). This is therefore a theory appealing to **A POSTERIORI** knowledge because we cannot know consequences without some experience of them. Utilitarianism is a theory of rational desire.

SITUATION ETHICS argues there is only one intrinsic good: **AGAPE** love. This is the highest form of love in Greek ethics - involving selfless love for stranger and friend. This highest good cannot be proved empirically, nor can we prove that it is "better" than, say, pursuing pleasure or happiness: rather it has to be accepted and followed (**POSITIVISM**). In other words, to prove its worth you first need to believe in the cause of love. It is quite wrong to call this pure relativism, and much better to see it as **PRINCIPLED RELATIVISM** (Fletcher's own term). This is because there is one absolute principle, **AGAPE** love, which cannot be broken. However, in applying this principle every choice must be made **RELATIVE** to circumstances and the creation of the most loving outcome. So in this latter sense, situation ethics is relativistic.

Situation Ethics is (like utilitarian teleology) a **CONSEQUENTIALIST** theory. This means that every act requires a calculation of consequences before the choice is made. Which choice maximises agape love? This will require a degree of practical wisdom to weigh consequences accurately.

2. HOW ARE THE THEORIES APPLIED?

RELATIVISTS see goodness as relative to culture or experience and so any situation needs to be applied to the relevant cultural value. These may still be very **REASONABLE** but, argues the relativist, even **REASON** is culturally conditioned.

UTILITARIANS see the right action as one that maximises happiness or pleasure. So we need to examine the likely consequences, count how many are affected by our choice, and then apply the Greatest Happiness Principle. We apply utilitarian principles **CONSEQUENTIALLY**. However, utilitarians still have the challenge of explaining why I should have a **DUTY** to consider the interests or happiness of others (even complete strangers) in my utilitarian calculation. Can utilitarian ethics escape from this essential **EGOISM** and partiality - that my happiness or possibly mine and my family's has greater weight than the **GENERAL** happiness.

Fletcher's **SITUATION ETHICS** applies the one intrinsic good, **AGAPE** love to different situation as in order to calculate the most loving outcome. Like utilitarian ethics, it therefore requires an empirical calculation. Here it is important to follow the four working principles, particularly **PERSONALISM** (put the individual first) and **PRAGMATISM** (take a case by case approach and weigh each case on its loving merits). Because Fletcher's theory fits firmly between legalism and antinomianism (that is, "no rules"), it avoids putting forward hard and fast rules on say abortion or euthanasia. The legalist for example would say abortion is absolutely wrong even when a victim is raped. The situationist would always favour an abortion in this and other cases where love's need (putting the mother first) was best served. Fletcher goes even further "it would be self-defence against not one, but two aggressors" (1966:39), the foetus and the rapist.

3. REALISM

How realistic are these theories from the perspective of modern sciences such as **PSYCHOLOGY** and **BIOLOGY**?

RELATIVISM fits well the postmodern world where there is no one overarching narrative accepted as true. It also fits **FREUDIAN** psychology where conscience comes from our upbringing and the sense of shame engendered by our parents and teachers. In the postmodern age we are taught to **TOLERATE** difference.

UTILITARIANISM suffers from the problem of application. Add a consequentialist ethic its usefulness depends on two things: the wisdom of the individual and the reliability of the facts in each calculation. Consider the war in Iraq: the facts (weapons of mass destruction) were false and the wisdom (that there would be few casualties) proved mistaken - the troubles roll on ten years after invasion. is it realistic to make this case by case calculation? Mill seems to concede that it is not when he argues for a form of weak **RULE UTILITARIANISM** (not his term, but JO Urmson's) which argues that we should take the wisdom of past generations and the rules which result, into account first and follow them unless a moral conflict between two "goods" occurs. Then we should revert to being **ACT UTILITARIANS**.

Moreover, it could be argued that **HAPPINESS** is too vague a goal, and as an end in itself it fades as soon as we attain its object, like a mirage. I buy the new car and find the satisfaction I was expecting fades very quickly. Happiness, it might be argued, is a by-product of something else and Mill again hints at this when he asks us "not to expect more from life than it is capable of bestowing."

For the **SITUATION ETHICIST** the problem is one of application.

AGAPE may be understandable (for example, we understand that the Good Samaritan in Luke's parable did something very noble), but the goal is so high that only Jesus himself attains it. Are we really to sacrifice the £2.50 I have in my pocket to the needy beggar under the arch, because love demands it? Most would say this is morality gone too far.

4. MOTIVATION - WHY BE MORAL?

So we come to the final, and perhaps most pressing question. Why be moral at all? Why not live a life of selfish egoism and be a parasite on the goodness of everyone else?

RELATIVISM is a wide and ambiguous concept. Joseph Fletcher (Situation Ethics) defined himself as a relativist (Situation Ethics is a form of **CHRISTIAN** relativism). He argued that we are moral out of love for fellow human beings. But this begs the question why I should bother about fellow human beings when it's not in my interest to do so. Fletcher's answer was that we need to convert to the way of love - commitment comes before action. He calls this **THEOLOGICAL POSITIVISM**. Situation ethics is something of a special case and is arguably not a pure form of relativism as it has one **ABSOLUTE** at its centre - agape love.

UTILITARIANS are not agreed on what motivates us. **BENTHAM** thought we were psychological **HEDONISTS** motivated by the prospect of pleasure and avoiding pain. **MILL** disagreed. He thought pleasure and happiness were not the same, as happiness needed clear goals and strenuous activities. Happiness is to be found in challenges met and difficulties overcome - which sometimes can involve discipline and sacrifice. Why bother with the happiness of others? Mill answered, out of **SYMPATHY** for my fellow human beings. "In the Golden Rule of Jesus of Nazareth ("do to others as you would have them do to you" Matthew

7:18)," wrote Mill, "is all the ethics of utility."

With **SITUATION ETHICS** Fletcher argues that we should be moral as a response to the love God first showed to us. He argues that love is not the preserve of the Christian - anyone can love sacrificially and atheists often do. But the Christian has a **REASON** to love - out of gratitude for what God first did for us. So Christian situation ethics is **EUCHARISTIC** (based on thanksgiving). The Christian alone has a deeper reason for loving.

> "In Christian ethics before we ask 'what shall I do?' we ask 'what has God done?'... not a scheme of living according to a code, but a continuous effort to relate love to a world of relativities." (1966: 157-8)

However, we might ask of Fletcher: "why should I be moral if I don't believe?." He seems to have no answer for this.

Exam Rescue Remedy

1. Build your own scaffolding which represents the logic of the theory. Use a mind map or a summary sheet.

2. Do an analysis of past questions by theme as well as by year. Try writing your own Philosophy of Religion paper based on what hasn't come up recently.

3. Examine examiners' reports for clues as to how to answer a question well.

4. Use the **AREA** approach suggested in this revision guide. **ARGUMENT**- Have I explained the argument (from Plato or Kant for example)? **RESPONSE** - Have I outlined and explained a good range of responses to the argument? **EVALUATION** - Now I have clearly set out positions, what do I think of these? Is mine **A PHILOSOPHICAL** argument and why? Does the original argument stand or fall against the criticisms raised? Why or why not?

5. List relevant technical vocabulary for inclusion in essay (eg efficient cause, form of the good, analytic, synthetic).

6. Prepare key quotes from selected key authors, original/contemporary. Learn some.

7. Contrast and then evaluate different views/theories/authors as some questions ask "which approach is best?" So contrast every approach with one other and decide beforehand what you think.

8. Practise writing for 35 minutes. Don't use a computer, unless you do so in the exam.

9. Always answer and discuss the exact question in front of you, never learn a "model answer." Use your own examples (newspapers, films, documentaries, real life). Be prepared to think creatively and adapt your knowledge to the question.

10. Conclude with your view, justify it (give reasons) especially with "discuss."

Lightning Source UK Ltd.
Milton Keynes UK
UKOW04f1204240314

228703UK00002B/2/P